WATCH OUT!

DEADLY POISONS ARE WAITING AROUND EVERY CORNER!

They're in your home...
and in the garden.
Shops are full of them!

FIND OUT...how to spot a deadly poison!

FIND OUT...how to save a poisoned person!

FIND OUT...how to beat deadly germs!

FIND OUT...how to beat the food scientists!

POISON POINTS

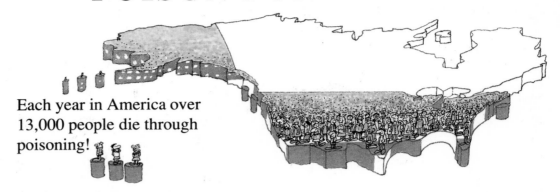

Each year in America over 13,000 people die through poisoning!

Boys are more likely to be accidentally poisoned than girls!

Years ago, kings and queens were afraid of being poisoned. So they used people called food-tasters who tasted the food to see if it was safe to eat.

POISON! BEWARE!

The best way to read this book is to begin at the beginning and read all the way through.

You'll be amazed at what you'll find out.

But if you want to read about one particular thing, such as spiders or food additives, look in the index on page 33.

Steve Skidmore wrote this book. He is a teacher and a writer for T.V.

Thompson Yardley drew the pictures.

ISBN 0 304 31774 8

First published in 1990 by
Cassell Publishers Limited
Artillery House, Artillery Row
London SW1P 1RT

Printed and bound in Great Britain
by MacLehose & Partners Ltd, Portsmouth

WHAT IS POISON?

Another word for poisonous is...

TOXIC

So if something is NON-TOXIC, it's not poisonous.
Most crayons are non-toxic in case young children chew them!

Watch out for the words
TOXIC and NON-TOXIC
on things around your house or school!

Look out for these symbols too...
You'll see them on packaging and on
labels. They both mean that the
contents are poisonous.

OLD-FASHIONED SYMBOL

MODERN SYMBOL

Poison works from inside the body...

So...HOW DOES IT GET IN?!

HOW POISONS ENTER YOUR BODY

BY BREATHING...

You can be poisoned by fumes from cars and factories.

THROUGH THE SKIN...

Poison can get into your skin just like water soaking into a sponge!
Some chemicals which gardeners use act like this. Be careful when you handle soil and plants.

THROUGH A HOLE IN THE SKIN...

Poisons get into the body through holes in the skin such as cuts or grazes.

HOW POISONS ENTER YOUR BODY

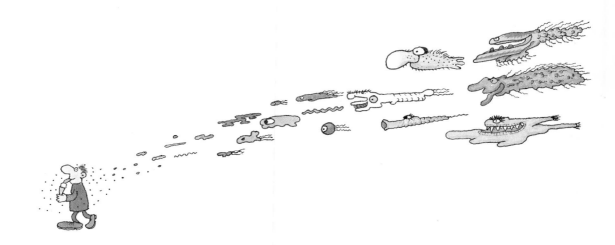

FROM GERMS...

Some germs which live in food give off deadly poisons.
Take a look at page 28...

I think I'll have a glass of lemonade!

BLEACH

BY SWALLOWING...

This is the most common way that people are poisoned.
It's easy to swallow poison by mistake, even in your own home.

Take a look..........

SPOT THE POISONS!

Here's an ordinary house.
How many of the numbered
items are poisonous?

BATHROOM

HOW TO STOP ACCIDENTAL POISONING...

There are two easy things to do:

1. Check that poisons are out of reach of young children. They might think they're good to eat or drink!
Make sure that all lids are on bottles and cans, and put them in a high cupboard...

...but not too high!

2. Never put poison into a bottle with the wrong label on it. Lots of people have been poisoned by weedkiller that's been stored in a lemonade bottle!

SPOT THE POISONS!

1 After-shave
2 Disinfectant
3 Paint
4 Paint-stripper
5 Carpet shampoo
6 Soap
7 Bubble bath liquid
8 Aspirin
9 Antiseptic

10 Lavatory cleaner
11 Animal medicines
12 Alcohol
13 Tobacco
14 Glue
15 Air freshener
16 Lighter fuel
17 Wax polish
18 Ammonia

19 Bleach
20 Washing-up liquid
21 Dyes
22 Old cat food
23 Washing powder
24 Shoe polish
25 Metal polish
26 Weed killer
27 Fertilizer

28 Insecticide
29 Rat poison
30 Brake fluid
31 Turpentine
32 Engine oil
33 Paraffin
34 Rust remover
35 Antifreeze
36 Petrol

KITCHEN

GARDEN SHED

Answer to **SPOT THE POISONS:** *All of them could poison you!*

7

MARY, MARY, QUITE CONTRARY...

1 **HONEYSUCKLE**

Poisonous berries.

2 **RHUBARB**

Poisonous leaves.

3 **GREEN POTATO**

Poisonous.

4 **DAFFODILS**

Poisonous bulbs.

5 **LUPINS**

Poisonous seeds.

6 **SPURGE LAUREL**

Poisonous berries.

7 **DEADLY NIGHTSHADE**

Deadly poisonous.

8 **MONK'S HOOD**

All parts are poisonous.

9 **BROOM**

Poisonous seeds and seed pods.

10 **YEW TREE**

Poisonous leaves and fruit.

11 **FOXGLOVE**

Deadly poisonous.

Most gardens have POISONOUS PLANTS growing in them. Here's a real horror-show garden...

12 **LAUREL**

Poisonous leaves and berries.

13 **HEMLOCK**

Poisonous leaves and seeds.

14 **POISON OAK**

Leaves are poisonous to touch.

15 **ROWAN TREE**

Poisonous berries.

16 **THORN APPLE**

All parts are poisonous.

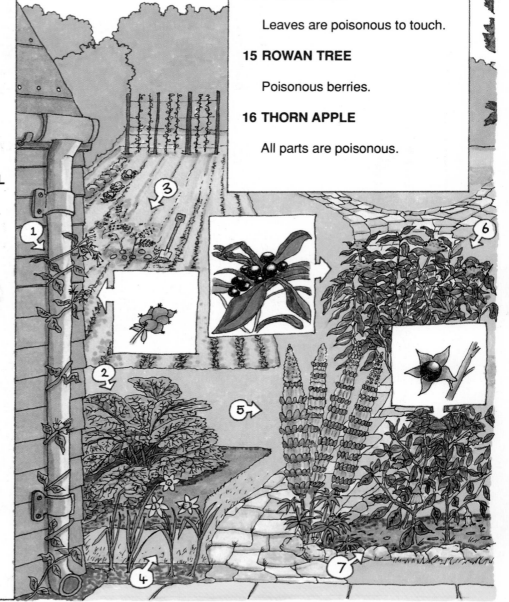

8

HOW DOES YOUR GARDEN GROW?

Very dangerously!

There are many more poisonous plants. Don't eat anything if you don't know what it is, especially FUNGI!..

MUSHROOMS AND TOADSTOOLS

Mushrooms and toadstools are called fungi.
There are thousands of different sorts of fungi.
Some are too small to be seen.
There could be one here!.......

Some fungi contain DEADLY POISONS!

WHAT HAPPENS IF YOU EAT THESE?..

DESTROYING ANGEL
Looks a lot like a mushroom from a greengrocer, but it's deadly poisonous!

DEATH CAP
No known cure for this one!
It causes nearly all of the deaths from mushroom poisoning!

FLY AGARIC
Not always deadly, but it makes you go mad!

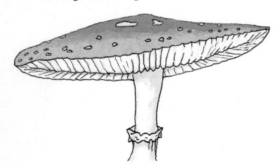

COMMON INK CAP
Good to eat except if you drink alcohol as well. Then it makes you sick!

Poisonous mushrooms often look like ones you can eat.
SO... it's best if you only eat mushrooms you buy from a shop.

**SPOT THE
DIFFERENCE...**

MUSHROOM   **TOADSTOOL**

They are both the same!

The word toadstool is often used to describe a mushroom that's poisonous.
BUT... some mushrooms can be poisonous too!
SO... If you're not sure, leave wild mushrooms and toadstools to the toads!

HELP A TOAD ACROSS THE ROAD

Here's a tired toad who needs a rest. See if you can guide him to his stool through the traffic. He mustn't touch any of the people or traffic or exhaust fumes!

Now you know what a toadstool is, find out about TOADFISH!..

CREATURES TO MAKE YOU SHUDDER AND SHAKE!

Lots of wild animals around the world are poisonous. All of these creatures are bad for your health if they get you!..

CENTIPEDES AND MILLIPEDES

Usually small and harmless, but some can bite through skin and poison you!

HORNETS

They look like large wasps and give a painful sting. If they gang up on you, they can be deadly!

VENOMOUS TOADFISH

Lives in the Atlantic Ocean and can grow up to 50cm long. It has poisonous spines!

STING RAY

Lives near the coasts of Europe, Africa and America. Has either one or two poisonous spines!

WEEVER FISH

It often buries itself in the sand on the sea-bed. It has poisonous spines, so it's very painful if you step on it!

CREATURES TO MAKE YOU SHUDDER AND SHAKE!

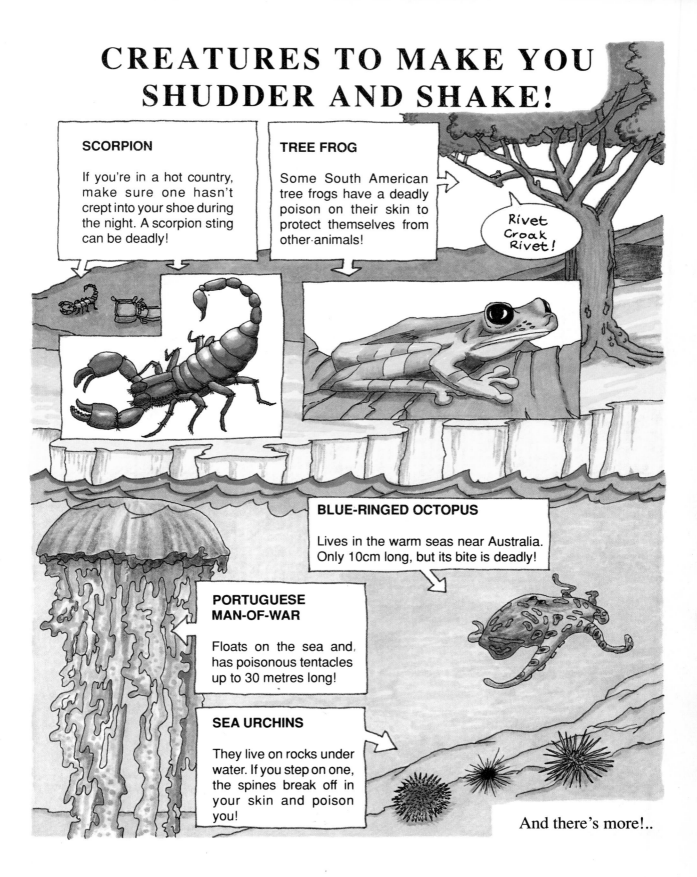

SCORPION

If you're in a hot country, make sure one hasn't crept into your shoe during the night. A scorpion sting can be deadly!

TREE FROG

Some South American tree frogs have a deadly poison on their skin to protect themselves from other animals!

Rivet Croak Rivet!

BLUE-RINGED OCTOPUS

Lives in the warm seas near Australia. Only 10cm long, but its bite is deadly!

PORTUGUESE MAN-OF-WAR

Floats on the sea and has poisonous tentacles up to 30 metres long!

SEA URCHINS

They live on rocks under water. If you step on one, the spines break off in your skin and poison you!

And there's more!..

ARE YOU SCARED OF
SPIDERS!?

Don't be! Most spiders are harmless to humans.

BUT...   there are a few which
have poisonous bites
which are deadly! If you
think you've been bitten
by one of those, it's best
if a doctor sees you.

TARANTULA
Found in tropical
parts of the world.
They have been
known to hide in
bunches of bananas,
so they can turn up
in cooler parts of the
world too!

FUNNEL WEB SPIDER
An Australian spider with
a killer bite. They like to
live in cobwebby tunnels
under stones and logs.

BLACK WIDOW
SPIDER
Found in warm areas all
over the world. Its bite
can be deadly.

When spiders bite,
they usually inject
a poison which
stops the victim
from moving, so
they can't escape.
Some spiders store
captured insects in
a sort of larder
made of cobwebs.

SNAKES!

Some snakes have hollow teeth so that they can inject their victims with poison.
Snake poison is called VENOM.

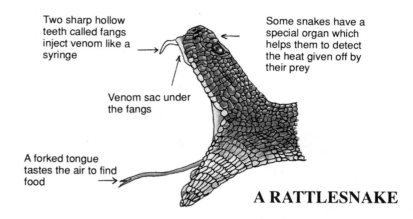

Two sharp hollow teeth called fangs inject venom like a syringe

Some snakes have a special organ which helps them to detect the heat given off by their prey

Venom sac under the fangs

HOW IT WORKS...

A forked tongue tastes the air to find food

A RATTLESNAKE

SNAKE FACT
Snakes don't sting, they bite!

SNAKE FACT
Many snakebites are harmless!

SNAKE FACT
Some snake venom can stop your heart!

If you're bitten by a snake... DON'T PANIC!

Don't rush about! Running makes the blood flow round your body more quickly. That means the venom will soon reach your heart. Try not to move the part that's been bitten. Somebody will have to bring a doctor to see you. There are cures for most snakebites.

zzzz!

YOW! A snake!

Some people die of fright when they are bitten by harmless snakes or wasps!

SO...GET TO KNOW YOUR SNAKES...

15

SNAKES AND ADDERS

HOW TO PLAY

1. You need a counter for each player and a dice.

2. Each player throws the dice in turn, and the first player to throw a six starts the game.

3. Move your counter along the board the same number of spaces as the score on the dice.

4. If you land on a snake you have to go to HOSPITAL.

5. The winner is the first player to get to the TONGUE TWISTER.

31 KRAIT

An Asian snake. Its bite often kills. 90-150cm long.

32

33
You put your fingers into the snake cage at the zoo. Move back 8 squares.

30

34

29

35 TAIPAN
Dangerous deadly snake from Australia.

28

66

67

If you have to move, walk as slowly as you can.

65 COPPERHEAD
From Eastern USA. 60-90cm long.

63
You try to trap a snake for fun. Move back 20 squares.

64

41
COBRA
Lives in dry rocky areas in Asia. 1.5-2m long.

26 **27** You stop somebody from teasing a trapped snake. Move to square 30.

40

36

19 **18**

25

37

39

Some snakes spit poison. You remember to wash it out of your eyes. Move to square 45.

38

Cutting open the bite may make it easier for the venom to get into the blood.

A very tight bandage will stop blood flow and can do more damage than the bite. A fairly tight bandage is enough to stop the venom spreading.

7

24

23

You go camping and remember to take a snake-bite kit with you. Move forward 3 squares.

22

21 TIGER SNAKE

Very poisonous. Lives in dry areas in Australia. 130-160cm long.

20

6

5

Your friend has been bitten by a snake, but you don't panic. Move to square 10.

1 **2**

SSSTART!

3

4 ADDER

Lives in moorland in Europe. 30 - 75cm long.

SNAKES AND ADDERS

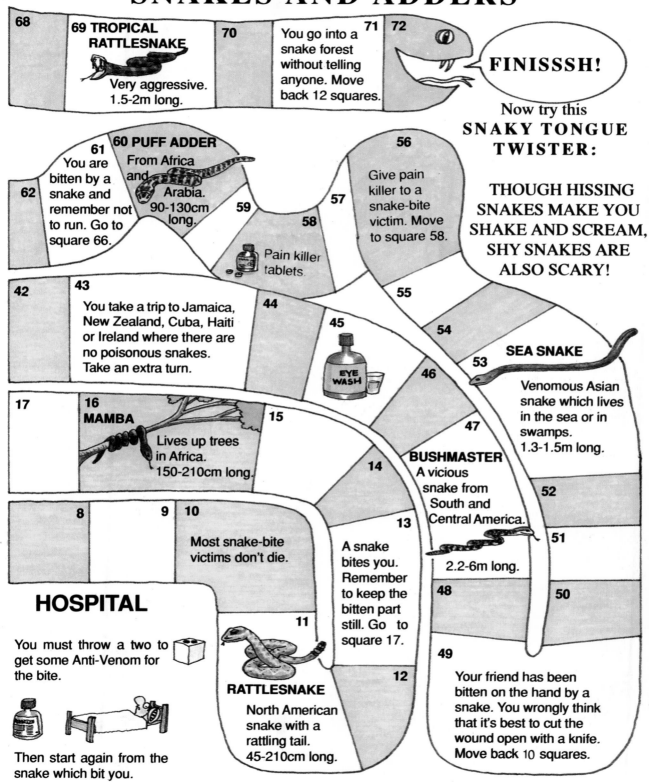

68

69 TROPICAL RATTLESNAKE
Very aggressive. 1.5-2m long.

70

71 You go into a snake forest without telling anyone. Move back 12 squares.

72

FINISSSH!

Now try this
SNAKY TONGUE TWISTER:

THOUGH HISSING SNAKES MAKE YOU SHAKE AND SCREAM, SHY SNAKES ARE ALSO SCARY!

61 You are bitten by a snake and remember not to run. Go to square 66.

60 PUFF ADDER
From Africa and Arabia. 90-130cm long.

62

59

58

57

56 Give pain killer to a snake-bite victim. Move to square 58.

Pain killer tablets.

42

43 You take a trip to Jamaica, New Zealand, Cuba, Haiti or Ireland where there are no poisonous snakes. Take an extra turn.

44

55

54

53

SEA SNAKE
Venomous Asian snake which lives in the sea or in swamps. 1.3-1.5m long.

45
EYE WASH

46

17

16 MAMBA
Lives up trees in Africa. 150-210cm long.

15

14

47

BUSHMASTER
A vicious snake from South and Central America. 2.2-6m long.

52

51

8

9

10 Most snake-bite victims don't die.

13 A snake bites you. Remember to keep the bitten part still. Go to square 17.

48

50

HOSPITAL

You must throw a two to get some Anti-Venom for the bite.

Then start again from the snake which bit you.

11

RATTLESNAKE
North American snake with a rattling tail. 45-210cm long.

12

49 Your friend has been bitten on the hand by a snake. You wrongly think that it's best to cut the wound open with a knife. Move back 10 squares.

Some crazy people poison themselves on purpose!..

TOBACCO

People who smoke
are poisoning themselves
with all sorts of terrible
toxic chemicals.

SO... smokers may get
any of these serious
illnesses...

Loss of senses
of taste and
smell

Bad breath

Heart disease

Ulcers and
stomach cancer

Weak muscles

Blood clots

Throat cancer

Bronchitis

Lung cancer

Bad blood
circulation

Empty wallet!

SPOT THE SMOKER
Which of these people smoke?

Whoof!
Whoof!

Being in the same room as
a smoker can be harmful
to you too!..

KOFF!

HOO!

GASP!

Answer to   **SPOT THE SMOKER:** *The one in the ambulance of course!*

FAG FACTS!..

Tobacco smoke makes clothes smell horrible!

It's against the law to sell tobacco to people under 16 years old in Britain and in most of Australia

Many house-fires are started by smokers leaving cigarette ends burning!

Tobacco smoke contains over 4,000 different chemicals. Many of these are poisonous! For example...

NICOTINE is one of the deadliest poisons in the world. It affects the heart and the nerves!

18,000 people die in Australia each year of illnesses caused by smoking tobacco **100,000 people die in Britain**

TAR is an evil-smelling brown substance which blocks up the lungs!

CARBON MONOXIDE replaces the oxygen in the blood so that smokers easily get out of breath!

Work out how much a 20-a-day smoker spends on tobacco in 30 years

Some people poison themselves twice, by smoking and by drinking alcohol!..

ALCOHOL

is a poison that people drink. It's in these drinks...

BEER
WINE
SPIRITS

ZZZZZ!

People who smoke often have to drink a lot to soothe their sore throats!

Alcohol can make you feel happy for a while, but it often makes you feel sick later on.

Alcohol makes you feel tired too!

Small amounts of alcohol aren't dangerous. Some health experts say that a glass of wine each day is good for you. BUT...drinking too much is bad for you...

SPOT THE DRUNK

One of these people drinks too much alcohol.
See if you can tell which one it is.

Alcohol changes people's behaviour. Quiet, harmless people can become violent if they drink too much!

Drinking too much alcohol makes people drive dangerously. That's why drinking and driving is against the law.

*Answer to **SPOT THE DRUNK**: The one being sick is the drunk!*

BOOZY BUSINESS

It's against the law to sell alcohol to people under 18 years old!

Alcohol is produced by the fungus called yeast. Just as some mushrooms make deadly poisons, yeast makes alcohol which can poison people who drink a lot!

Alcohol can damage the blood vessels in your skin so that some people who drink too much get a big red nose!

Mine's bigger than yours!

Your liver helps to remove poisons from your body by cleaning the blood. Alcohol can damage the liver so that it doesn't work properly. That means that the blood becomes clogged up with other poisons too!

Some people lose their memory after drinking a lot of alcohol!

Alcohol can destroy brain cells!

Alcohol drinkers in the United States of America spend about 45 billion dollars a year on beer, wine and spirits!

eek!

Alcohol can damage blood vessels in your leg. Then your toes might drop off!

Alcohol is addictive. That means that some people can't do without it. They have to get medical help to stop drinking.

Other things are addictive too!..

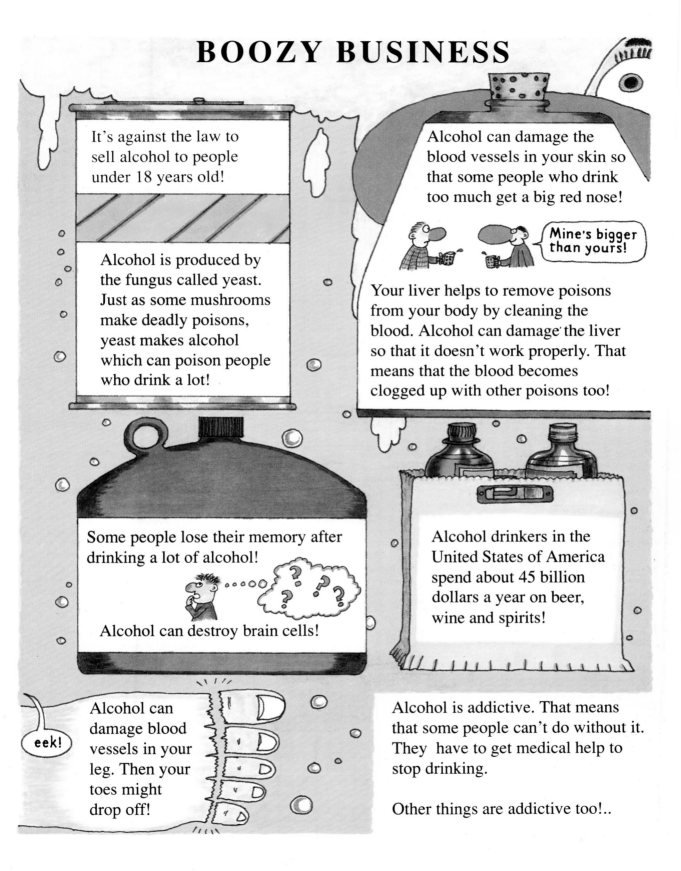

21

DRUGS

Drugs are substances which affect the body. They are often used by doctors as pain killers or to help cure a patient. Most drugs are poisonous if used wrongly, even those which doctors give to their patients.

BUT...some drugs are too dangerous to use at all. SO...it's against the law to use them.

Here are four dangerous drugs which are banned by law.

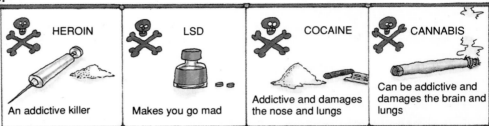

HEROIN — An addictive killer

LSD — Makes you go mad

COCAINE — Addictive and damages the nose and lungs

CANNABIS — Can be addictive and damages the brain and lungs

SPOT THE DRUG-TAKER

Which two of these people use drugs which are against the law?

Banned drugs can also contain all sorts of other poisons! This is because they are produced and sold by people who don't care about other people's lives.

The Drug Police in America once found a stash of cannabis that was mixed with HORSE MANURE!

*Answer to **SPOT THE DRUG-TAKER:***
The one who thinks she can fly and the one robbing somebody to get money to buy drugs!

DEADLY DRUG DATA

DRUG DEALERS

People who sell unlawful drugs often give them away free at first. They do this to get their customers addicted to drugs. Then they can charge whatever price they like.
Beware of older children giving away sweets!

GLUE SNIFFING

Sniffing glue damages the lungs and the nose. It also makes people stupid by damaging the brain!

COST

Some heroin addicts need a week's wages every day to pay for their habit!

SOLVENT ABUSE

In Britain, it's against the law to sell solvents such as cellulose paint thinner to people under 16 years old!

MENTAL HEALTH

Most mental hospitals have patients who are there because they have used banned drugs which have made them ill!

COCAINE

Cocaine damages the delicate parts of the nose. Cocaine addicts often have runny noses!

ACID

LSD makes users see things which aren't there. Sometimes they think that they're being chased by HORRIBLE MONSTERS!

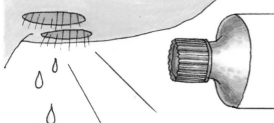

HOUSEHOLD DRUGS

Always keep drugs in the right containers and away from little children. Some quite ordinary drugs can be fatal!

SNACKS AND ADDITIVES

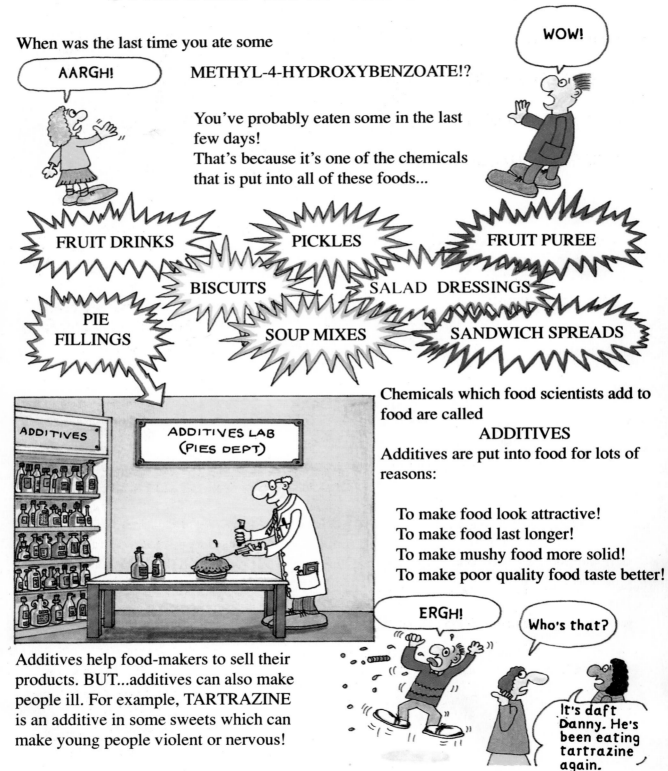

When was the last time you ate some

AARGH!

METHYL-4-HYDROXYBENZOATE!?

WOW!

You've probably eaten some in the last few days!
That's because it's one of the chemicals that is put into all of these foods...

FRUIT DRINKS

PICKLES

FRUIT PUREE

BISCUITS

SALAD DRESSINGS

PIE FILLINGS

SOUP MIXES

SANDWICH SPREADS

ADDITIVES

ADDITIVES LAB (PIES DEPT)

Chemicals which food scientists add to food are called
ADDITIVES
Additives are put into food for lots of reasons:

To make food look attractive!
To make food last longer!
To make mushy food more solid!
To make poor quality food taste better!

ERGH!

Who's that?

Additives help food-makers to sell their products. BUT...additives can also make people ill. For example, TARTRAZINE is an additive in some sweets which can make young people violent or nervous!

It's daft Danny. He's been eating tartrazine again.

SNACKS AND ADDITIVES

Some additives can give you

SKIN RASHES

STOMACH UPSETS

TROUBLE WITH BREATHING

In Europe, all additives are given an E-number. For example, E123 is called Amaranth. This additive gives some people rashes.

There are hundreds of different additives. Not all of them are bad for you. Sweets often have lots of additives in them. Here's a label from a stick of rock with eight E-numbers in it!

E-number	NAME	PROBLEMS
E102	Tartrazine	Rashes, nervousness and breathing problems
E110	Sunset Yellow	Rashes and headaches
E123	Amaranth	Rashes
E124	Ponceau	Breathing problems
E127	Erythrosine	Sensitivity to light
E132	Indigo Carmine	Sickness and rashes
E142	Acid Brilliant Green	Breathing problems and rashes
E153	Carbon Black	Thought to be connected with cancer

LITTLEGOODNESS ROCK

CONTAINS: SUGAR, COLOURS, E102, E110, E123, E124, E127, E132, E142, E153.

The more additives you eat, the more likely you are to be poisoned.
Have a look around your house for lists of additives on packages.
Don't be poisoned. Avoid additives when you can!

25

HOW TO EAT GERMS

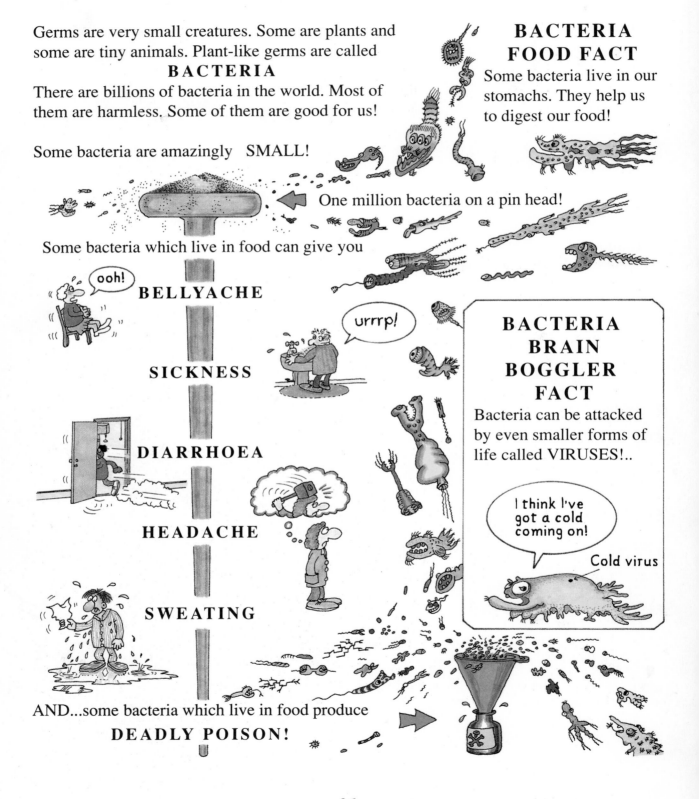

Germs are very small creatures. Some are plants and some are tiny animals. Plant-like germs are called
BACTERIA
There are billions of bacteria in the world. Most of them are harmless. Some of them are good for us!

Some bacteria are amazingly SMALL!

BACTERIA FOOD FACT
Some bacteria live in our stomachs. They help us to digest our food!

One million bacteria on a pin head!

Some bacteria which live in food can give you

ooh!

BELLYACHE

urrrp!

SICKNESS

BACTERIA BRAIN BOGGLER FACT
Bacteria can be attacked by even smaller forms of life called VIRUSES!..

DIARRHOEA

HEADACHE

I think I've got a cold coming on!

Cold virus

SWEATING

AND...some bacteria which live in food produce
DEADLY POISON!

HOW TO EAT GERMS

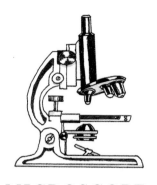

MICROSCOPE

Bacteria are so small that you need a microscope to see them. This works like a powerful magnifying glass.

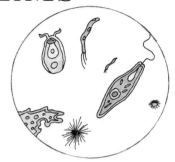

VIEW DOWN A MICROSCOPE

Here are some ways that food can be invaded by bacteria.

Blah Blah!

Blah Blah!

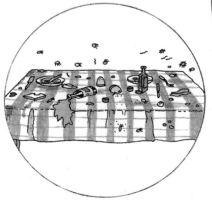

Boing!

WHAT TO DO...

HOW TO BEAT GERMS!...

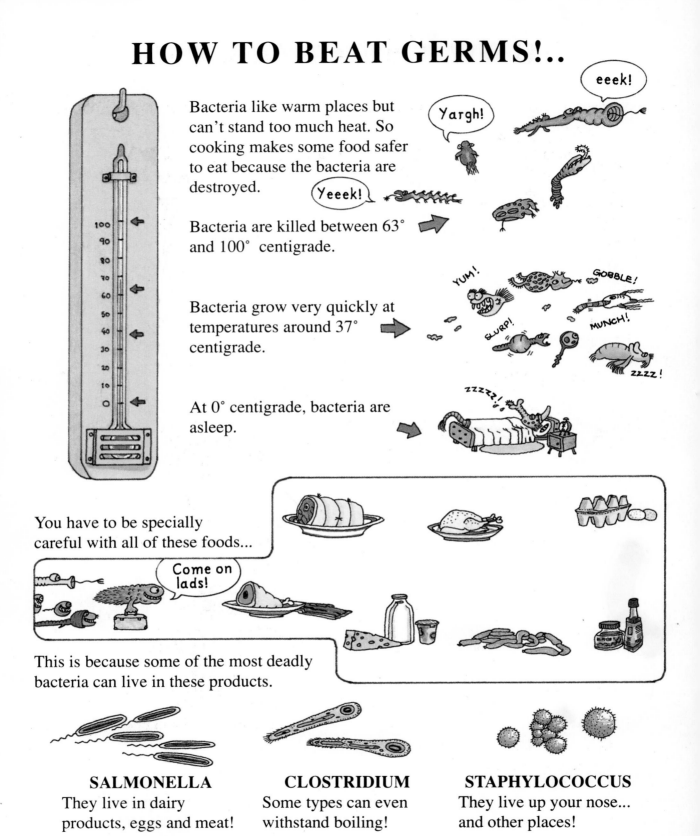

Bacteria like warm places but can't stand too much heat. So cooking makes some food safer to eat because the bacteria are destroyed.

Yargh!

eeek!

Yeeek!

Bacteria are killed between 63° and 100° centigrade.

Bacteria grow very quickly at temperatures around 37° centigrade.

YUM!

GOBBLE!

SLURP!

MUNCH!

ZZZZ!

At 0° centigrade, bacteria are asleep.

ZZZZZ!

You have to be specially careful with all of these foods...

Come on lads!

This is because some of the most deadly bacteria can live in these products.

SALMONELLA
They live in dairy products, eggs and meat!

CLOSTRIDIUM
Some types can even withstand boiling!

STAPHYLOCOCCUS
They live up your nose... and other places!

HOW TO BEAT GERMS!..

Here are a few basic rules which will help you to cut down the risk of food poisoning:

Wash your hands before touching food!

Don't just warm up leftovers! Leftovers must be cooked properly!

Keep all of your kitchen tools and surfaces clean! Use hot soapy water!

Make sure that frozen food is thawed out before you cook it!

Make sure that food is properly cooked before you eat it!

Don't store cooked and raw meat together!

LOOK! If you spot anyone breaking these rules, leap into action and save yourselves and others from deadly poisons.

HOW TO BE A LIFE-SAVER

It's not easy to tell if somebody's been poisoned.
BUT...there are some clues.

WHAT TO LOOK FOR

A poison such as mushrooms, weedkiller or aspirin is nearby or...
The person's mouth might be stained or...
The person is asleep and can't be woken up.

WHAT TO DO

If the person is asleep and can't be woken up...

1. DON'T PANIC!
2. Call a doctor straight away!
3. Take out anything that's loose in the person's mouth so that they don't choke. That includes false teeth!
4. Save any poison you find nearby to show the doctor!
5. Don't try to make the person sick!
6. Try to get the person into the recovery position if you are strong enough!
7. Keep the person warm and comfortable!

SEE PAGE 31 FOR THE RECOVERY POSITION

If the person is awake...

1. DON'T PANIC!
2. Call a doctor straight away!
3. Give the poisoned person lots of water or milk to drink!
4. Keep the person awake, warm and comfortable!
5. Save any poison you find nearby to show the doctor!

HOW TO BE A LIFE-SAVER

THE RECOVERY POSITION

Lying in the recovery position is the best way for a sleeping person to breathe.

Sleeping people are almost impossible to move. Don't try too long before you call a doctor.

Here are two more poisons you can save people from...

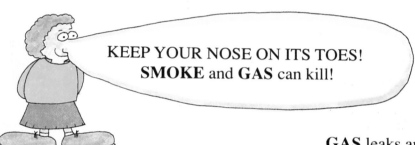

KEEP YOUR NOSE ON ITS TOES!
SMOKE and **GAS** can kill!

SMOKE from house-fires is deadly dangerous! When soft furniture catches fire, the smoke given off is a killer. If you can smell it, you're already being poisoned!

A damp cloth will stop some of the smoke or gas from reaching your lungs.

GAS leaks are deadly! If you smell gas in your house **DON'T LIGHT A MATCH OR SWITCH ON A LIGHT!** It might cause an explosion!

WHAT TO DO

GET OUT
and call for the Gas Company

There's lots more to know about First Aid. Go and see your local Red Cross branch or First Aid Group to find out!

WHAT TO DO

GET OUT
and call for the Fire Brigade

The Ace Poison Spotter says...

DON'T PUT THINGS
YOU AREN'T SURE ABOUT
IN YOUR MOUTH!

You'll probably see some of the poisons in this book every day. Some are a lot less common.

BUT...now that you're an expert on poisons, you'll be safe from most of them!

AND...you'll know when to leap into action to save other people's insides!

ONE MORE THING...

DON'T EAT THIS BOOK!
IT MAY BE
POISONOUS!

INDEX